INTRODUCTION

Since 1960, Gordon S. Clausen has given hundreds of carpet maintenance clinics and seminars nationally. He has taught at Cornell University Hotel School and has served as consultant to the American Hotel-Motel Association. Frequently the audience asked if the information was available in print. Until now, it was not.

Mr. Clausen graduated from The Wharton School of the University of Pennsylvania, and The Philadelphia Textile Institute. He has spent twenty years as a textile engineer administering carpet mill production and twenty years in its maintenance.

He is presently president of Clausen Marketing Associates, a leading manufacturer of carpet maintenance chemicals with plants in Philadelphia, Atlanta, Dallas, Chicago and Los Angeles.

Reinecke Associates
Box 3112
West Chester, PA 19380

CARPET

PROCUREMENT & MAINTENANCE

FOR THE
NINETIES

By: Gordon S. Clausen

TABLE OF CONTENTS

CHAPTER I

THE HISTORY OF CARPET

In order to properly maintain on-location wall-to-wall carpet, it is essential that the maintenance personnel be completely familiar with carpet construction and fibers. It is important to know the type of construction, and often, it is the determining factor in choosing the maintenance method. Therefore, Chapter One will be devoted to carpet so that the best possible maintenance is performed by the maintenance personnel.

There are two major types of carpet manufactured, woven and tufted. Woven carpet is manufactured on carpet looms where all of the yarns, such as pile yarns, stuffer yarns and backing yarns are fed into the loom at one time and become woven carpet. The three major types of woven carpet are 1) Wilton, 2) Velvet and 3) Axminster. Both Wilton and Velvet are available in loop or cut pile, while Axminster is available in cut pile only.

Tufted carpet is the most important method for manufacturing carpet today. The tufting machine mimics a mammoth sewing machine with hundreds of needles. Each needle eye is threaded with yarn and is moved through a backing fabric. A loop or tuft is formed as the needle is pulled out, and is held in place by the backing fabric. In order to anchor the tufts permanently in place, a heavy coating of latex is applied to the back of the fabric. Tufted carpet is available in both loop and cut pile. Loop pile means that surface yarns are woven into the body of the fabric and left uncut. Cut pile means the face of the carpet is composed of cut ends of the pile yarn.

In order to give tufted carpet stability (dimensional) a second backing is applied at the carpet mill. Choice of second backings may be rubber, jute, vinyl or polypropylene. Our survey shows the present trend is to use polypropylene both as the primary and secondary backing. It is also known as olefin. This makes modern day carpet impervious to damage from possible overwetting, using cleaning methods that might previously have been harmful to the animal and vegetable fibers, formerly used in carpets. Tufted carpet has replaced woven carpet because the tufting machines operate so much faster than weaving looms. Hence the labor costs have been greatly reduced and passed on in the pricing of the carpet.

Because of its high cost and impracticability the manufacture of wool carpet yarn has been reduced to a very small amount, and replaced with synthetic carpet fibers. The leading pile yarn used today for commercial carpet is continuous filament nylon. However, many other synthetics are successfully used, such as staple nylon, polypropylene (olefin) polyester, acrylics and cotton. The primary backing into which the pile yarn is tufted is principally woven or non-woven polypropylene. Besides polypropylene, secondary backings may be rubber, jute or vinyl. Since tufted carpet predominates the sales of carpet today, we will eliminate buying specifications for woven carpets. Specifications for the procurement of tufted carpet include: 1) GAUGE—this measures the closeness of construction along the width of the tufting machine. A six gauge carpet which would be lower priced household construction, identifies as six tufts per inch. An eight gauge carpet which is most household carpet and some commercial carpet is identified as eight tufts per inch. Ten gauge carpet which identifies as ten tufts per inch is the best possible commercial construction. Twelve gauge has been used for certain specialty types of carpet.

STITCH: While the gauge measures across the tufting machine, the stitch measures the amount of times the needles punch the pile yarn into the primary backing. Eight stitch is approximately the maximum in tufted construction, therefore, if a carpet is eight gauge, eight stitch, it

8

would have sixty-four tufts per square inch. It is recommended that for commercial use a maximum of fifty-six tufts per square inch be used.

PILE WEIGHT: Pile weight is determined by the amount of pile yarn in one square yard. A simple gauge to use: under twenty ounce is low quality, twenty ounce to thirty-six ounce would be medium pile weight, and thirty-six ounce to sixty ounce would be heavy duty pile weight. Please bear in mind for good maintenance and appearance, a closer construction (ten gauge) of forty ounce pile weight would serve much better than a looser construction (six or eight gauge) with a sixty ounce pile weight. Total weight per square yard consists of the pile weight, the primary backing, the secondary backing and the adhesive used to adhere the two backings.

PILE HEIGHT: A one inch height of pile is called one-thousand, therefore, one-half inch is five-hundred and one-quarter of an inch is two-hundred-fifty. A two-hundred-fifty height of pile in a ten gauge carpet with a forty ounce pile weight will wear better, maintain its appearance after maintenance and resist pile crushing and shading in commercial use. A more expensive half inch pile weight in an eight gauge construction with sixty ounce pile weight, would be less satisfactory. While many commercial installations of carpet use cut pile, the greatest retention of appearance and lack of pile shading proves loop or uncut pile construction serves commercial use best. Uncut or loop pile is usually in buildings with heavy traffic such as airports, schools and hospitals. For service in various traffic areas, the following specifications should meet most requirements for commercial use, and since loop pile does not shade or crush, nor lose its twist factor, we recommend loop over cut pile. It should also be noted that with the introduction of many new fibers on the market today, it is possible there are other variations of carpets constructed that will withstand the rigors of severe traffic.

9

CARPET SPECIFICATIONS:

Heavy Duty Traffic: Approximate specifications—10 gauge, 8 stitch, 34–50 ounce continuous filament nylon pile weight, .200–.250 height of pile. Tufted in primary polypropylene with woven polypropylene secondary back and a 14–20 pound tuft bind.

Moderate Duty Traffic: 8 gauge, 7–8 stitch, 28–34 ounce continuous filament nylon pile weight. Tufted in primary and secondary polypropylene back, .150–.200 height of pile.

Light Duty Traffic: 8 gauge, 6 stitch, 22–26 ounce continuous filament nylon pile weight, tufted in primary and secondary polypropylene back, .150 height of pile.

Scratch Test: While carpet specifications may sound complicated, there is a very simple means for the novice to determine quality. Loose samples or laid carpet should be scratched as harshly as possible with a finger nail. Penetration of the pile reaching the primary backing is virtually impossible in an excellent quality carpet. A medium quality carpet gives much resistance in reaching the primary backing when using this test. On a low quality carpet, penetration takes place instantly, and the finger dwells on the primary backing. Therefore, the scratch test many times will determine the maintenance method to be used. Bear in mind that if the finger nail can penetrate the pile, that the maintenance machines and chemicals also can. It is highly recommended that if the scratch test proves the carpet to be of low quality, the maintenance personnel should check further to determine the fibers used in the backing yarns.

If the primary and secondary backings are polypropylene, overwetting damage is impossible. If jute, which has a burlap appearance, is in the backing yarns, caution must be taken not to overwet in the cleaning procedure. Polypropylene accepts no water, hence causes no dimensional change which can occur in jute.

CARPET TILES

It is highly recommended if an institution is considering installing carpet tiles (18") in preference to broadloom carpet, that they buy and install loop or uncut pile tiles in preference to cut pile construction. Also they should buy three color tweeds or designs in preference to solid color tiles.

See cleaning procedure page 28.

Some useful carpet terms and their meanings would be as follows:

BROADLOOM—Any carpet woven or tufted seamless on a broad-loom in widths of 54" or more. Broadloom does not refer to any brand, grade or quality, nor to any specific weave.

CONTINUOUS FILAMENT NYLON—Nylon composed of long continuous strands of fiber.

CUT PILE—The face of carpet which is composed of cut ends of pile yarn.

GAUGE—The distance between two needle points expressed in fractions of an inch.

HEAT-SET NYLON—A thermosetting resin that can be cross-linked by heat to form a three-dimensional mold that holds its shape.

LOOP PILE—The surface yarns of a woven fabric in which the loops are woven into the body and left uncut.

OLEFINS—Any long chain synthetic polymer composed of at least 85% weight of ethylene, polypropylene or other olefin units. Polypropylene makes an excellent fiber for primary and secondary backings, due to its lack of moisture acceptance, therefore eliminating overwetting hazards such as shrinkage or seam popping.

PILE CRUSH—Bending of pile by constant walking or the pressure of furniture. (More prevalent in cut pile than loop pile)

PILE HEIGHT—The height of pile measured from the top

surface of the back to the top surface of the pile.

SHADING—Bending or crushing the surface fibers so that the sides of the fibers reflect the light. Viewed from one direction of the rug or carpet, the crushed area will appear darker in color, from the opposite side it will seem lighter. However, it is to be pointed out that the phenomenon of shading is inherent and characteristic of all pile fabrics, especially cut pile and it is not a defect.

STAPLE NYLON—Nylon composed of specially engineered fibers cut into short staple for spinning yarns.

INSTALLATION

There are two major means of installation used today. Commercial buildings such as airports, hospitals, schools, office buildings are installing double backed tufted carpet with direct gluedown and no underpadding. Most hotels and motels as well as homes are mostly installing carpet over underpadding with a tackless stripping installation.

CHAPTER II

ON-LOCATION CARPET CLEANING WHAT'S NEW IN CARPET AND ITS MAINTENANCE

The following is a reprint of an article which appeared in the March 1986 issue of *Maintenance Supplies Magazine* as written by the author.

WHAT'S NEW IN CARPET AND ITS MAINTENANCE!

1950's

What's New in carpet maintenance starts in the early 50's. The only means of on-location carpet cleaning at that time was to use a rotary floor machine with a solution tank and channel back brush. Previous to 1950, coconut oil shampoos were the only available on-location cleaning chemicals. Then, in the early 50's, the first sudsing synthetic detergents were introduced for carpet shampooing with the advantages over coconut oil shampoo in that they were fully soluble in water to give an even cleaning solution, and did not create the bad resoiling condition produced from coconut oil shampoos. At the same time, in the household cleaning field, Glamorene introduced the first powder dry cleaner. Housewives made Glamorene an instant success but commercial results were minimal due to high labor cost, the heavy soil on commercial carpet and other problems involved in using powders in institutions. Glamorene in the 80's discontinued manufacturing powders and now manufactures only liquid carpet cleaners.

1960's

In the 50's and 60's most carpet was manufactured using wool (animal fibre) as a pile yarn and cotton and jute (vegetable fibres) as stuffer and backing yarns. When overwetting from rotary shampooing, problems could arise such as shrinkage, seam popping, and dry rot of backing yarns. To overcome these problems in rotary liquid shampooing, dry foam carpet cleaning machines were introduced. Dry foam machines immediately became very popular in buildings doing in-house cleaning due to the lack of problems possibly created in rotary shampooing. However, professional carpet cleaners and contract cleaners found foam machines did not perform as well as rotary machines on heavily soiled carpets creating the problem that foam cleaning was more of a maintainer and must be performed more often creating a higher labor cost. For this same high cost of labor and lack of performance the professionals did not use powder dry cleaning as well as not using foam cleaning.

In the 1960's the chemical manufacturers added additional ingredients to the synthetic detergent shampoos such as 1. Brighteners (optical), 2. Soil retardants (DuPont Ludex), 3. Dry foams for dry foam machines.

1970's

In the 1970's and 1980's, carpet manufacturing was completely changed from woven carpets using wool, cotton, and jute to the manufacturing of needle tufted carpets using nylon (90%) and other synthetic pile yarns as well as polypropylene primary backing materials and now in the 1980's using polypropylene secondary backings. Gone are the animal and vegetable fibres with their problems such as shrinkage, seam popping and rotting. Now any wet cleaning method can be used without fear of damage to the carpet. Polypropylene is the perfect primary and secondary fibre for carpet as it accepts no moisture, therefore, eliminating *old bugaboos and scare copy of doing damage to carpet in wet cleaning methods.*

This change in carpet manufacturing was perfect timing for the introduction of hot water extraction cleaning known as steam cleaning. Today 90% of new carpet cleaning equipment is extraction machines. Self- contained units having mixing tanks and recovery tanks were introduced in a variety of capacities and variety of PSI and waterlift. The first cleaning tools, called Wands, gave way to brush head extraction units that jet the chemicals and water into the carpet then brush to the surface the soil and dirty water to be extracted by the vacuum shoe.

New extraction cleaning chemicals were introduced with sudsless emulsions of synthetic detergents and dry cleaning solvents along with defoamers to kill the suds in the recovery tanks.

1980's

Hot water extraction machines with brush heads continue to totally dominate on-location carpet cleaning. However, in the 80's automatic carpet machines were introduced that work similar to automatic floor scrubbers. Their fast operation at low labor costs indicate that in the future all areas of large carpet installations such as schools, hospitals, office buildings, airports, football fields, etc. will be forced into using automatic carpet cleaning machines.

Introduced in the late 70's and 80's for interim cleaning of heavy duty areas of carpet such as entrance ways, elevators, walkoff mats, etc. is a new method called rotary bonnet buffing. This is a very low cost means of first aid appearance in between extraction cleaning. Any rotary machine is equipped with a pad driver and carpet bonnets. For instant drying the carpet and bonnet are sprayed with a diluted solution of sudsless detergents and dry cleaning solvents then the carpet is buffed. For even better cleaning results, if one hour drying time is allowable, the bonnet is submerged in the diluted chemicals, then squeegeed before buffing. Using one chemical, one machine, and one labor step this system is excellent with the lowest total cost possible.

With the 1980's producing new viruses, bacteria and contagious diseases such as Aids, Legionaires disease and Kawasaki Syndrome, necessary breakthrough was essen-

15

tial in the chemical maintenance of carpet.

No longer is carpet cleaning *ONLY* satisfactory in hospitals, nursing homes, schools and restaurants, etc. Something must be done about germs in order to protect patients, school children, customers, etc. In order to manufacture chemicals that claim anything to do with germs the product must be submitted to EPA and, if approved, assigned an EPA Registration Number.

First maintenance people must understand the classification of EPA Registrations for carpet chemicals:

1. *STERILIZE*—Completely kills all micro organisms including spores, bacteria, virus and fungi. Not available for carpet EPA Registration.

2. *GERMICIDAL* OR *DISINFECT*—Kills all bacteria and certain viruses and fungi. Not available for carpet EPA Registration.

3. *SANITIZE*—Substantially reduces bacteria by 90% plus in carpet. Not a complete kill. Available for EPA Registration in a cleaner or as a spray after cleaning has been performed.

4. *GERMASTAT* OR *BACTERIASTAT*—Prevents the regrowth of germs during the cleaning and dry drying cycle only. No kill claim. Available for EPA Registration in a cleaner or as a spray after cleaning.

Fortunately, in 1986 some carpet cleaners on the market for hot water extraction machines and rotary bonnet buffing have now received EPA Registration Numbers for CLEANING, SANITIZING AND DEODORIZING all in one chemical cleaning operation at no additional cost of labor, machines or chemicals.

Quaternary Ammonium Compounds which are added to carpet cleaners to qualify for EPA Registration sanitizing require the presence of water and moisture in the cleaning operation. This means powder dry cleaners could not qualify to sanitize carpet.

CHAPTER III

PRESENT DAY CARPET CLEANING METHODS & COSTS SPOTTING CHART

O n-location carpet cleaning is divided into three distinct stages: 1) Spot and spillage maintenance 2) Frequent maintenance of the heavy traffic areas between overall cleaning and 3) cleaning of the entire carpeted area. The spotting chart on page 24 will explain the major types of spillage and methods of treating these problems.

It is imperative that people responsible for carpet maintenance understand the terminology of pH. pH is the chemical means of measuring alkalinity and acidity. Number seven is neutral. Anything from seven through twelve is alkaline. Below seven is acid. All carpet fibers are dyed with hot acids at a low pH. Therefore, all carpet is on the acid side. Most carpet spotters of the detergent type are alkaline and are used to remove acid stains. To remove alkaline stains that show up as browning from overwetting, cleaning and flooding or leaking from air conditioners, etc. use synthetic citric acids sold under names identified as non-browning alkaline removing chemicals.

Interim Carpet Cleaning Methods:

The major means of cleaning heavy traffic areas such as entrances, elevators, walk-off mats, etc., is rotary bonnet buffing. This is a very simple method utilizing any rotary floor machine, with a pad driver holding a carpet bonnet for buffing. Carpet bonnets are preferred for this use, compared to nylon or polyester floor pads, since the bonnets absorb the surface soil and create heat which shortens any drying time.

Regular floor machines that run at 175 RPMs can safely be used for rotary shampooing with flag tipped nylon brush bristles, or carpet bonnets. High speed machines of 300

RPMs or more should not be used for shampooing six gauge carpet or polypropylene pile yarn.

High speed bonnet buffing should be restricted to loop or uncut pile construction of eight or ten gauge carpet. Twist factor reduction can occur in high speed shampooing or buffing of cut pile carpet.

It is recommended that you try all types of bonnets on your carpet, to determine which type of bonnet most successfully performs on your selected carpet construction. While bonnet buffing does an excellent surface cleaning, the soft spinning bonnet does not remove deeply imbedded soil between the tufts. This type of soil is only removed with brush head hot water extraction machines. The following three methods have been used effectively. 1) For instant drying, the bonnet and carpet are sprayed with the diluted chemicals, and the carpet is then buffed. 2) If an hour drying time can be allotted, better bonnet buffing will be achieved by using the submerged bonnet buffing system. 3) The third bonnet buffing method is used and recommended by **MR. CHRISTOPHER J. HILL, MANAGER FOR HARVEY'S RESORT HOTEL & CASINO IN LAKE TAHOE, NEVADA.** In order to save labor time and cut costs they have devised a method to eliminate spraying or submerging of the bonnets. One man quickly bonnet buffs as follows: They use a rotary floor machine with a solution tank, into which they pour a sudless solution of solvents and detergents. For buffing, they restrict full release of the diluted cleaner by partially closing the valve at the bottom of the solution tank in order not to overwet the carpet for quick drying. Under the housing of the rotary machine is a flow through stiff bristle bonnet holder, to which the bonnet is attached until dirty. The operator in the one step cleaning operation uses several bonnets.

For best performance, the chemical requirements would be as follows: The cleaner must be sudless so as to avoid the unnecessary labor costs of removing suds by vacuuming. The chemicals should consist of solvents and detergents which cut the oily soil residual, holding the soil to the carpet tufts. There are presently Environmental Protection Agency approved products for bonnet buffing, that in addition to cleaning, and at the same chemical and labor costs will sanitize and deodorize the carpet. At times, powder dry cleaners have been used for interim maintenance.

Some carpet mills consider it adequate for carpet tiles, since it might eliminate overwetting in the hands of a novice. However, the cleaning results do not compare to bonnet buffing, and the costs are prohibitive when costs are a factor. We quote **MR. JOSEPH FORTNER, FACILITY SUPERVISOR OF THE CUPERTINO, CALIFORNIA DIVISION OF HEWLETT-PACKARD.** When his company installed carpet tiles, the manufacturer recommended they maintain the carpet tiles by using powder dry cleaners. They purchased dry cleaning equipment and chemicals, only to find the cleaning results were very poor and the many labor steps required made this method prohibitive costwise. "We no longer use powder dry cleaning equipment and chemicals. Our carpet tiles are now maintained weekly and monthly by rotary bonnet buffing (submerged method) utilizing sudless solvent detergent chemcials. Periodically, we hot water extract the carpet tiles with power brush heads attached to self-contained extraction machines. Our carpet appearance has greatly improved at a much less maintenance cost."

Overall Carpet Cleaning:

There are many types of overall carpet cleaning methods utilized today. They are rotary shampooing, foam shampooing, extraction self-contained units, extraction automatic cleaning machines, powder dry cleaning and cylindrical brush surface cleaning. The advantages and disadvantages of each method are listed in the comparison of carpet cleaning methods on the next page. This comparison of methods and costs does not include the cost of removing furniture and is based on $4.50 an hour labor cost which may vary in other parts of the country, and are only used as a guide.

The square foot cleaning cost of each method is determined by three factors: 1) the cost of the chemicals used, 2) the amount of and cost of machines used and 3) the amount of labor steps required. The least expensive methods for areas of tremendous footage are automatic extraction machines. The reason for the extreme low cost of automatic extraction cleaning is the footage cleaned per hour. After moving furniture, vacuuming, and using all of the other on-location methods, 400–600 feet per hour can be cleaned. When run on #1, or deep cleaning speed, the automatic method cleaned 3,000 feet per hour, or when used for pile surface maintenance and fast drying cleaned 6,000 feet per hour. This tremendous production speaks for itself, and the cleaning costs are based on two to three cents per square foot. These machines use two chemicals, extraction cleaner and defoamer, plus one labor step, depending on the selection of speed at which the machine is operated determines the cost of .02 per ft. or .03 per ft.

In contrast, powder dry cleaning when used on heavily soiled carpet will require a liquid prespray and a labor step to apply, to be followed by three additional labor steps. Number one is the hand spreading of the powder, two is the running of the application machine, and three, when the powder is dry, the physical vacuuming of the carpet. The use of two chemicals and four labor steps create a cleaning cost of 17 to 20 cents per square foot. This is why a professional carpet cleaner or a professional cleaning contractor very rarely offers powder dry cleaning, since they cannot charge enough to make this cleaning system profitable.

Quoting

MR. ROBERT G. FRIEDMAN, VICE-PRESIDENT, SALES & MARKETING PACIFIC FLOOR MACHINE COMPANY
FORMER NATIONAL SALES MANAGER, CLARKE FLOOR MACHINE COMPANY
DIVISION OF COOPER INDUSTRIES
STATES:
"Demonstrations with wet cleaning systems, such as hot water extraction or rotary shampooing, are far more dramatic and thorough than dry cleaning systems. The wet methods flush out the dirt in the carpet and deep clean, thereby, reducing the rate of resoiling of the carpet."

CARPET TILES
Your author recently served as a consultant to two very large hospitals, each having installed approximately one and one half years ago, over 200,000 square feet of cut pile solid color carpet tiles.

Each hospital now finds themselves in the exact same dilemma. The carpet is badly shaded and pile crushed causing an undesirable appearance because each hospital selected cut pile instead of loop pile. They also installed solid colors which now appear heavily soiled as well as shaded and pile crushed. Both hospitals in future installations will use loop pile carpet tiles in multiple color tweeds and designs.

Also both hospitals are discontinuing the use of powder dry cleaning chemicals and equipment, as recommended by the tile manufacturer. They are now using rotary bonnet buffing for interim maintenance and hot water extraction for periodic deep cleaning. For both methods they are using EPA registered carpet chemicals that in one step, 1.) Cleans, 2.) Sanitizes 90%, plus kill of germs and bacteria as well as 3.) Deodorizes the carpet.

SPOTTING CHART

Oil & Greasy Spots Butter, oil, grease, hand cream, ballpoint pen ink, asphalt, crayon, foundation makeup, hair oil, furniture polish, mascara, paint (latex, paint [oil-base]), shoe polish, typewriter ribbon.

Procedure
Remove excess material, apply solvent spotter, dry carpet. Repeat if necessary. Brush pile gently after drying. Use pile fibre cloths to apply solvents. *Do not spray directly into the carpet.*

Oily Foodstuffs, Animal Matter
Coffee, tea, salad dressing, milk, ice cream, gravy, sauces, egg, chocolate, vomit, blood, heavy grease, catsup, cheese, earth (dirt), excrement, mayonnaise, toothpaste, starch, white glue.

Remove excess material, apply solvent spotter, then apply all-purpose spotter. Use pile fibre cloths, then a brush or sponge for the 8 pH solvent-detergent all-purpose spotter.

Foodstuffs, Starches, Sugars
Candy, soft drinks, alcoholic beverages. Stains: fruit, washable ink, urine, excre-ment brown water stains.

Blot up liquids and scrape off semi-solids. Apply all purpose spotter. If necessary reapply all purpose spotter. Brush pile gently or vacuum after drying.

Rust Spots
Rust spots from any source

Apply rust remover, then shampoo to neutralize rust remover

Chewing Gum

Apply aerosol chewing gum remover

Candle Wax

Apply steam from steam iron to melt wax. Place heavy brown kraft paper on melted wax, then apply iron to paper to absorb wax onto the paper.

24

SPOTTING CHART

Spotting

The Procedures

Remove spots as soon as they are discovered. Some spots may discolor the carpet, if they are not treated soon enough. Before you start general shampooing, pre-treat spots as follows:

1. Blot up any liquid with pile fabric cloth or paper towel, scrape any solids with a dull knife.

2. For spots of unknown origin, always use a solvent spotter first, then if needed use an all-purpose spotter. Reason: If the spot is greasy, a detergent type remover may spread the grease. Apply solvent spotter to a cloth, not directly into the carpet pile.

3. Grease, oil, tar or gum-based stains are removed with a solvent cleaner.

4. Protein and sugar-based spots need a detergent spotter.

NOTE:

To eliminate musty, urine, vomit and all organic odors, add two ounces of a water based deodorant to each gallon of diluted carpet shampoo, or squirt several drops directly on the carpet. A quaternary ammonia Environmental Protective Agency registered product performs most satisfactorily, especially on mildew odors.

It should also be noted that powder dry cleaners do cleaning only. With the ever present new viruses, bacteria germs, etc., in the future, cleaning only will be insufficient. To register an Environmental Protective Agency product for sanitizing it must contain quaternary ammonia. The germicidal benefits of this product will work with water only. Hence, powder dry cleaners cannot receive an Environmental Protective Agency registration for sanitizing and cleaning in one chemical application, with the same labor and chemical costs.

Many contractors state they can make more money and clean the carpet better when quoting 10¢ a foot for hot water extraction, than when quoting 20¢ a foot for powder dry cleaners.

Today, it is estimated that 90% of on-location carpet cleaning is performed by the two leading methods of rotary bonnet buffing and hot water extraction. The other 10% would be composed of other methods utilizing such systems as rotary shampooing, foam shampooing, powder dry cleaning, or twin brush washing. Following are some interesting quotations from the vice-presidents of two of the county's largest and leading carpet maintenance supply distributors:

CHARLES LANE, Vice-president of National Sanitary Supply Company, which is the largest sanitary maintenance distributor in the country, states: "Over ninety percent of the carpet cleaning equipment and chemicals (not including vacuums) are sold for use in the two leading on-location carpet cleaning methods, rotary bonnet buffing for interim maintenance of carpet, and hot water extraction for periodic deep cleaning." National Sanitary Supply has two hundred and eighty–five sales persons operating in a five state marketing area of California, Nevada, Arizona, Utah and New Mexico.

EASTERDAY SUPPLY COMPANY is also one of the largest sanitary maintenance product distributors in the country, utilizing over one-hundred salesmen in their major markets of San Francisco, Los Angeles, Reno, Sacramento, Palm Springs, San Jose and Anchorage, Alaska. We quote **IRVING WINTER, VICE-PRESIDENT:** "Ninety-five percent of sales for carpet maintenance are for equipment and chemicals used in rotary bonnet buffing and hot water extraction, including automatic extraction machines." Easterday specializes in carpet maintenance equipment and chemicals for all types of carpet cleaning.

In the procurement of hot water extraction equipment, self-contained units comprising mixing tanks and recovering tanks are available in various sizes. Since the most expensive labor factor in extraction cleaning is down time of the machine, while disposing of the recovery, it is recommended for buildings with large areas of carpet to buy the largest capacity self-contained units available. If carpet cleaning is performed in a small motel, funeral parlor, bowling alley, etc., smaller units would be more practical.

PSI is the term given to the pressure per inch in which the diluted chemicals are forced into the carpet. Self contained units vary from one manufacturer to the other and some manufacturers today make available machines with a variable PSI ranging from 50–200. It is highly recommended that when cleaning six gauge carpet, especially if there is any jute or cotton in the primary or secondary backings to not use more than 50 PSI. If the carpet is eight or ten gauge construction, and consists of polypropylene primary and secondary backings, there is no fear of damage to the carpet from overwetting by going to a higher PSI pressure.

Johnson Research Div.,
Johnson Advertising Assoc.,
Wayne, Pa.

June 1, 1985

NOTE: BEFORE ANY METHOD IS USED — DRY VACUUMING IS NECESSARY
COMPARISON OF CARPET CLEANING METHODS ON LOCATION

NOTE: This study does not include furniture moving—and is based on a labor cost of $4.50 per hour.

	ROTARY SHAMPOOING		FOAM SHAMPOOING		ROTARY BONNET BUFFING		ONE STEP	EXTRACTION		POWDER DRY CLEANING	TWIN BRUSH CYLINDRICAL BRUSH SURFACE CLEANING
	LOOP PILE	CUT PILE & PILE SET BY BRUSH AFTER SHAMPOOING	FOAM CLEAN ONLY	FOAM CLEAN WITH WET VAC FOLLOW-UP	SPRAY METHOD	SUBMERGE METHOD		SELF CONTAINED UNIT WITH BRUSH HEAD	AUTOMATIC CLEANING MACHINE	STEPS 1 LIQUID PRE-SPRAY 2 SPRINKLE POWDER 3 POWDER MACHINE OPER. 4 VACUUM POWDER	
MACHINES REQUIRED	1	1	1	2	1	1	1	1	1	2	1
NUMBER CHEMICALS REQUIRED	1	1	1	1	1	1	1	2	2	2	1
LABOR STEPS	1	2	1	2	2	2	1	1	1	4	2
DRYING TIME	4-10 hrs.	4-10 hrs.	1-2 hrs.	1-2 hrs.	0	½-1 hr.	½-1 hr.	2-4 hrs.	1-3 hrs.	½-1 hr.	½-1 hr.
COST PER SQ. FT. AFTER FURNITURE IS REMOVED. INCLUDING CHEMICALS, EQUIPMENT, & LABOR	.06	.08	.06	.08	.03	.04	.025	.06	.02-.04 According to Speed of Machine	.17	.04
	1 Chemical 1 Labor Step	1 Chemical 2 Labor Steps	1 Chemical 1 Labor Step	1 Chemical 2 Labor Steps	1 Chemical 2 Labor Steps	1 Chemical 2 Labor Steps	1 Chemical 1 Labor Step	2 Chemicals 1 Labor Step	2 Chemicals 1 Labor Step	2 Chemicals 4 Labor Steps	1 Chemical 2 Labor Steps
ADVANTAGES	Excellent Cleaning Ease of Maneuvering. Superior cleaning when extraction machine is combined with an acid rinse.		Short Drying Time. No Possible Damage to Carpet. Good Cleaning		No Drying Time. Inexpensive. Good Surface First Aid	Short Drying Time. Inexpensive. Excellent Surface Cleaning	Short Drying Time. Lowest Cost. Excellent Surface Cleaning	Excellent Cleaning Rinsing & Removal of Dirt. Water & Detergents for Lowest Rate of Resoiling	Duplicates in Plant Loose Rug Cleaning	No Wetting of Carpet	Good Surface Cleaning Low Cost
DISADVANTAGES	4-10 hrs. Long Drying Time. Possibility of Over Wetting. Detergent Build-up Recommend Occasional Extraction Rinse		Use as a Maintainer— Not Deep Cleaning. Possible Streaking of Carpet If Machine Not Properly Maintained		Pile Surface Cleaning Only	Pile Surface Cleaning Only	Pile Surface Cleaning Only	Cannot Use High PSI on Low Grade Carpet. 6 Gauge		Poor Cleaning Results Prohibitive Expense with 2 Chemicals & 4 Labor Steps. Collection of Powder in Loosely Constructed Pile Damages Yarn & Affects Wearability	
CHEMICAL BENEFITS	Cleaning Only		Cleaning Only		Cleaning, Plus EPA Registered Sanitizing & Deodorizing in One Chemical Application		Same as Other Two Methods	Cleaning Plus EPA Registered Sanitizing & Deodorizing in One Chemical Operation		Cleaning Only	Cleaning Plus EPA Registered Sanitizing & Deodorizing in 1 Chemical Operation
	Rotary Shampooing		Foam Shampooing		Rotary Bonnet Buffing			Extraction		Powder Dry Clean	Twin Brush

28

CHAPTER IV

PROCUREMENT SPECIFICATIONS FOR CARPET CHEMICALS

The following is a reprint from *Services Magazine,* January 1985. This magazine is the official publication of the Building Services Contractor Association. The article gives very technical chemical information on the types of various chemicals found in carpet cleaning products. It should be noted that hot water extraction chemicals clean at a 10–12 pH range, compared to most shampoos that clean at an 8 pH range. Cleaning personnel must be careful when cleaning light colored carpets such as beiges, off-whites and pale shades, with the extraction method used. It is possible to cause browning and oxidize these light colors when used in conjunction with high alkaline cleaners. To prevent alkaline browning when cleaning light colored carpet, it is recommended adding two ounces of synthetic citric acid (sold as a non-browning product) to a diluted gallon of extraction cleaner. If used within two hours, the acid which is harmless to the skin will not affect the cleaning ability of the detergents, solvents or the sanitizing of the Environmental Protection Agency approved quaternary ammonias. However, the cleaner containing the non-browning acid will not properly perform unless used within two hours.

With the exception of solvent spotters, all carpet cleaning products including detergent spotters, shampoos and extraction cleaners, are water based emulsions. The chemical activity or solids and the amount of water, as well as the quality of the detergents determine the price of the product. Every maintenance person knows that a 24% floor finish that contains 76% water is more expensive than a 12% finish that contains 88% water. In procuring carpet chemicals, the active ingredients should be specified, the same as they are specified in floor finishes.

Properties and make-up of carpet cleaning chemicals
By Gordon S. Clausen

Carpet maintenance chemistry has greatly changed in the past 30 years. Thirty years ago the only chemicals necessary for on-location carpet maintenance were solvent and detergent spotters and a carpet shampoo. The latter was composed of coconut oil, to be used in the only system available—rotary machine shampooing, a system which is still in use today.

As new methods and machines for on-location carpet maintenance were developed, it was necessary for the chemical manufacturers to keep pace and develop new chemical formulations necessary for each system.

Synthetic detergents

Probably the biggest change in the 1950's was the development of synthetic detergents to replace the old coconut oil shampoos. While coconut oil shampooing in a rotary machine produced visually satisfactory cleaning, there were several drawbacks:

1. The coconut oil shampoo was not fully soluble in water, hence causing a diluted solution that did not always produce even cleaning.

2. Without on-location rinsing or extraction, which was unknown at that time, coconut oil shampooing created a heavy, oily residue in the carpet that caused a serious resoiling problem. Once new carpet was shampooed, it never seemed to look as good as originally and also resoiled rapidly.

In addition to the coconut oil problem, another factor was also responsible for this. For many years, the channel back brushes used in rotary shampooing were too stiffly bristled and hence caused reduction of the twist factor in the plying of the pile yarn. This twist reduction caused blossoming of the pile yarn and a different appearance than when originally installed. Thus, I highly recommend a flagged tip nylon bristle be used in the channel back brush for all rotary shampooing.

To properly understand the synthetic revolution it is necessary to have some technical knowledge of the types of synthetic detergents available.

Types of surfactants

There are three classifications of surfactants used in formulating carpet cleaning solutions:

1. Anionic, which produces a negative charge.
2. Nonionic, which has no physical charge.
3. Cationic, which produces a positive charge. For good cleaning results it is possible to blend a cationic with a nonionic but cleaning results would be poor if an anionic (negative) were added to a cationic (positive) charge.

In order to overcome the objections of coconut oil shampoo for rotary shampooing, the most common ingredient in rotary foam shampoo "dry foam" is sodium lauryl sulfate (also known as sodium dodecyl sulfate). It is in the category of anionic surfactants called sodium alkyl sulfates. Its advantages are that it produces a dry foam which doesn't wet through to the carpet backing and is a high relatively stable foamer. Its disadvantage is that it leaves a waxy or tacky residue on the carpet which causes resoiling. Modifiers are added to produce a drier, more powdery, friable residue which is more easily removed in dry vacuuming when the carpet has dried. Also, any residue not removed in vacuuming will not attract dirt and cause resoiling.

My company has found that sodium lauryl sarcosinate is a good modifier. Polymers such as acrylics and styrene/maleic anhydride co-polymer give an even drier foam than sarcosinates and a more powdery residue, and are considered the Cadillacs of modifiers. Builder salts and solvents are added to aid in removing greasy soil, chelating agents to improve hard water stability, and optical brighteners to aid in retaining the color appearance of the carpet.

Chemicals for steam cleaners

When carpet extraction equipment, commonly known as steam cleaners, was developed, once again new chemicals had to be formulated. In extraction cleaning chemicals, the primary surfactant is generally a nonionic surfactant modified to make it low-foaming in hot water. In general, nonionic surfactants are moderate to low foamers and the only foam generated breaks down rapidly. Builders salts, optical brighteners, and solvents are also added to this type of cleaner. Dry residues are not a problem in this system since a very small amount of cleaner is used (two to four ounces per gallon of hot water). About 80 percent of the cleaner injected into the carpet is removed by vacuum extraction.

Bonnet buffing

While carpet shampoos and steam cleaners were developed to handle the requirements of rotary, reel foam, and extraction machines a very popular means of interim cleaning—the bonnet system—was developed and offered at a very low machine investment cost. Most contractors already had rotary machines, so all they had to buy in order to bonnet buff their carpets (similar to spray buffing of hard floors) were carpet bonnets and a pad driver to fit their rotary machine. These bonnets are thick, carpet-like products composed of cotton and synthetic fibre blends and are not to be confused with nylon or polyester floor pads.

Since rotary bonnet buffing, or a brand new system utilizing a Twin Brush machine, are interim systems used frequently to clean the heavy traffic areas in between the use of the overall systems already mentioned, it has the following chemical requirements:

1. It should not create suds, so as to avoid the need of a wet suction machine.

2. There must be a high proportion of solvents to cut the greasy soil and attract it to the bonnet, thus eliminating steam cleaners from this method as they contain more

detergents than solvents.

Therefore, the ideal sudsless cleaner to use is one composed heavily of solvents, but with the addition of detergents to clean all types of soil in the carpet and attract the soil to the bonnet. Quick drying, low equipment investment, and inexpensive labor cost have made the system the predominant interim system used in the United States. However, it is still surface first aid and does not eliminate the necessity of the overall cleaning systems, when required, according to the type and color of the carpet, the traffic to which the carpet is subjected, and the level of cleaning appearance needed.

In addition to the cleaning machine chemicals already discussed, there are several other carpet chemicals required that a contractor must know how to use:

1. All-purpose detergent spotters.
2. Solvent spotters to remove grease, tar, and oil.
3. Chewing gum removers.
4. Rust removers.
5. Anti-static sprays.
6. Carpet protector sprays.
7. Carpet deodorants.
8. Non-browning solutions to prevent oxidation (browning) or to remove it from carpet that has oxidized.

All contractors who use hard floor maintenance chemicals are familiar with the need to use only those germicidal floor cleaners registered with the EPA. However, for years the EPA would not register any products for use on carpet. There were no standard testing methods, and even today the EPA has not registered any germicidal carpet cleaner.

However, the EPA has finally accepted and registered sanitizing and deodorizing sprays to be used after cleaning, and has now registered the first sanitizing, deodorizing carpet steam cleaner (or extraction cleaner). Now it is possible to clean, sanitize and deodorize the carpet in one step, using a carpet extraction machine. The chemical developed by my company for this purpose contains a proprietary blend of nonionic, cationic, and amphoteric surfactants which readily emulsifies greasy and other soils without the need for solvents.

This type of product sanitizes with cationic quaternanes which destroy odor causing bacteria and also eliminates other odors with the inclusion of odor counteractants.

You will also find useful the following Carpet Chemical Buying Specifications written for the Portland, Oregon School System, in June of 1985. These specifications will give you excellent cleaning with the highest chemical activity and the slowest possible rate of resoiling. The finest carpet cleaning is achieved with a combination of solvents to cut the grease and detergents to clean the fibers.

CARPET CHEMICAL BUYING SPECIFICATIONS
Carpet Hot Water Extraction Chemicals
(Steam Cleaning)
(Two Types of Cleaners)

1. ① Active Ingredients—23.0 ± 1.0%
2. Percent Detergents—18.0 ± 1.0%
3. Basic Type of Detergents—Nonionic Surfactant Modified to Produce Low Foam in Hot Water
4. Percent Solvents—3.0 ± 1.0%
5. Basic Type of Solvents—Glycol Ethers and Water Soluble Alcohols
6. Type of Odor—Mild Solvent
7. Viscosity—3.0 ± 1.0 Centipoise (Brookfield LVF, 60 RPM, 70°F)
8. Flash Point—No Flash to Boiling (T.C.C.)
9. Other Ingredients—Builders, Coupling Agents, Optical Brighteners, Defoamers, Water Softening Agents, Preservatives, Fragrance, Water
10. Dilution Use: 2 Oz. Per Gal. of Hot Water
11. Shelf Life: 1 Year
12. pH 12.5 (+ Or –0.5)

Or ① EPA Registered—Sanitizing—Deodorizing Cleaner
Carpet Extraction Concentrate

1. ① Active Ingredients—14.0 ± 1.0%
2. Percent Detergents & Odor Counteractants—8.0 ± 1.0%
3. Basic Type of Detergents—Blend of Nonionic, Amphoteric and Cationic Surfactants
4. Percent Quaternary Ammonium Chlorides—2.0%
5. EPA Registration—Yes
6. Type of Odor—Pleasant, Characteristic of Odor Counteractants
7. Viscosity—5 ± 2 Centipoise (Brookfield LVF, 60 RPM 72°F)
8. Flash Point—None to Boiling (T.C.C.)
9. Other Ingredients—Builders, Water Softening Agents, Defoamers, Optical Brighteners, Water
10. Dilution Use—2 Oz. Per Gal. of Hot Water
11. Shelf Life—1 Year
12. pH 12.5 (+ Or –0.5)

Defoamer

1. Active Ingredients—25.0 ± 2.0%
2. Percentage Detergents—N/A
3. Basic Type of Active Ingredients—Silicone Defoamer Emulsion
4. Percent Solvent—N/A
5. Basic Type of Solvents—Glycol Ethers and Water Soluble Alcohols
6. Type of Odor—Nearly Odorless
7. Viscosity—10 ± 3 CPS (Brookfield LVF, 60 RPM, 72°F)
8. Flash Point—None to Boiling (T.C.C.)
9. Other Ingredients—Emulsifiers, Preservatives, Water

10. Dilution—1 Oz. Per Gal. Capacity of Recovery Tank
11. Shelf Life: 1 Year
12. pH 7.0 (+ Or –1)

Carpet Rotary Bonnet Buffing
Spray Or Immersion Method
(Two Types of Cleaners)

1. ① Active Ingredients—60 ± 2%
2. Percent Detergents—16 ± 2%
3. Basic Type of Detergents—Sodium Lauryl Sulfate, Sodium Alkyl Ether Sulfate, Sodium Alkylbenzene Sulfonate, Alkyl Alkanolamide
4. Percent Solvents—45 ± 2%
5. Basic Type of Solvents—Aliphatic Hydrocarbons and Glycolethers
6. Type of Odor—Floral Solvent
7. Viscosity—10 ± 5 Centipoise (Brookfield LVF, 60 RPM, 72°F)
8. Combustible
9. Flash Point—125°F (T.C.C.)
10. Other Ingredients—Builders, Coupling Agents, Water Softening Agents, Optical Brighteners, Fragrance, Water
11. Dilution Use: 8 Parts Water to 1 Part Cleaner
12. Self Life: 1 Year
13. pH 9.0 (+ Or –0.5)

Or ① EPA Registered—Sanitizing—
Deodorizing Cleaner
For Rotary Bonnet Buffing

1. Active Ingredients—14.0 ± 1.0%
2. Percent Detergents & Odor Counteractants—8.0 ± 1.0% Basic Type of Detergents—Blend of Nonionic, Amphoteric and Cationic Surfactants
3. Percent Quaternary Ammonium Chlorides—2.0%

4. EPA Registration—Yes
5. Type of Odor—Pleasant, Characteristic of Odor Counteractants
6. Viscosity—5 ± 2 Centipoise (Breakfield LVF, 60 RPM 72°F)
7. Flash Point— None to Boiling (T.C.C.)
8. Other Ingredients—Builders, Water Softening Agents, Defoamers, Optical Brighteners, Water
9. Dilution—For Rotary Bonnet Buffing Use—6 Parts Water to 1 Part Cleaner
10. Shelf Life—1 Year
11. pH 12.5 (+ Or –0.5)

**Carpet Rotary Shampooing Or Real Foam
Shampooing
Rug and Upholstery Shampoo**

1. ① Active Ingredients—20.0 ± 1.0%
2. Percent Detergents—16.0 ± 1.0%
3. Basic Type of Detergents—Product Shall Contain Sodium Lauryl Sulfate and A Modifier (Sodium Lauroyl Sarcosinate) to Reduce the Tackiness of the Sodium Lauryl Sulfate and Product a Dry Friable Residue. The Ratio of the Sodium Lauryl Sulfate to Sarcosinate Shall Be a Maximum of 3:1
4. Percent Solvents—4.0 ± 1.0%
5. Basic Type of Solvents—Glycol Ethers
6. Type of Odor—Fruity/Solvent
7. Viscosity—20 ± 10 Centipoise (Brookfield, LVF, 60 RMP 72°F)
8. Flash Point—None to Boiling (T.C.C)
9. Other Ingredients—Builders, Optical Brighteners, Preservatives, Fragrance, Water
10. Dilution Use: Light Soil 24–1 Dilution Use: Heavy Soil 16–1
11. Shelf Life: 1 Year
12. pH 8.0 (+ Or –0.5)

CHAPTER V

SURVEY OF CARPET MANUFACTURERS

Recently, Reinecke Associates surveyed over one hundred of the country's leading carpet mills pertaining to their knowledge of carpet cleaning methods, machines, chemicals and their recommendations. Some of the mills would give no recommendations of cleaning methods, because they felt they could not control the method used. Most of the mills recommended hot water extraction cleaning as well as powder dry cleaning. **PETER RACZES,** Manager of Commercial Claims of one of the major manufacturers, Mohasco Carpet Corp. (Mohawk, Alexander Smith and Firth) stated that the cleaning procedure depended on the individual situation which would include; dry extraction, hot water extraction, rotary brush method and the spin bonnet method. However, no procedure is recommended by brand name by Mohasco Carpet Corp.

Two very interesting factors were determined from this survey. On the question, "Does the carpet mill know the cleaning cost of the various methods available today?", fifty percent knew and answered "yes." This apparently means that the others had no conception of carpet cleaning costs. While some recommended powder dry cleaning, they were unaware that they were recommending a cleaning system that far exceeds the cleaning costs of their competition, tile floors. All of the carpet mills were familiar with the following cleaning methods: rotary shampooing, foam cleaning, hot water extraction and powder dry cleaning. Very few of the carpet mills had any concept of rotary bonnet buffing or automatic carpet extraction cleaning. This presents a strange situation in that the cleaning contractors and professional rug cleaners are using methods that the leading sanitary supply distributors are selling them and is 90% of their sales, and the carpet mills are unfamiliar with these methods.

If one were to watch most school or airport carpet cleaning today, they would find bonnet buffing being used in the heavy traffic areas on a nightly and weekly basis and hot water extraction on a periodic basis.

We suggest the reader be cautious in accepting the advertising of the manufacturers of the various carpet maintenance systems. Recently we read an advertisement for a system that stated "Recommended by all leading carpet mills." Reinecke Associates in surveying the leading carpet mills has received letters from many of them stating that they recommend no cleaning systems by name. Most carpet mills surveyed recommend two—four type systems, depending on the individual situation.

The answer from Reinecke's survey of over one hundred carpet mills, showed the highest percentage of carpet mills recommended hot water extraction cleaning of carpet. However, many of them also recommended rotary liquid shampooing, rotary bonnet buffing, foam cleaning, and powder dry cleaning. While most of these leading mills do not recommend any cleaning procedure by name, they do state the system used is dependent on individual situations.

CHAPTER VI

CARPET MAINTENANCE PROGRAM

It is impossible to set up a standard maintenance program for all carpeted areas since there are so many variable factors to be considered. The maintenance program factors to be aware of are: 1) The construction of the carpet, and in particular if the pile is a cut or loop weave. 2) The color of the carpet is of vital importance. For least costly maintenance, it is highly recommended that the pile yarn be composed of three different colors; a light shade, a medium shade and a dark shade. These three colors can be in the same color tones, such as beige, brown and cocoa, or they can be in contrasting colors, as long as they are light, medium and dark colors. Carpet selected in light colors only require a greater maintenance cost, while carpets selected in dark colors only require much more vacuuming. This is due to the more conspicious lint, spillage, cigarette ashes, etc., which are much more evident in a dark color. 3) Of extreme importance in setting up a maintenance program is the amount of traffic to which the carpet is subjected. Hence they are classified as heavy, medium, or light traffic areas. 4) The maintenance program is also determined by the desired level of appearance that the management considers satisfactory.

All maintenance programs are composed of four steps: 1) Vacuuming—it is recommended that upright vacuums have two motors, one driving the beater brush and the other vacuuming the loose soil. Also highly used, are one motor portable direct suction vacuums moving a large amount of air. Top loader vacuums should always be specified for commercial vacuuming. Vacuums range from 12 inches to 32 inches in width, with the selection being determined by the size of the areas to be vacuumed. For weight and flexibility, 12 to 16 inch vacuums should be used in smaller type areas such as hotel rooms and classrooms, whereas wide vacuums should be used in open large volume areas of carpet, such as hallways, lobbies, aisles, etc.

2) Removal of spillage, to eliminate the possibility of stain. Residual should be removed as promptly as possible by first using a dull knife to remove any solids on the carpet, or by using absorbent toweling to absorb any liquid that has been spilled. Chemical treatments thereafter would be in accordance with the spotting chart found in Chapter III.

3) Interim maintenance of heavy traffic areas in-between overall deep cleaning. These heavy traffic areas would be places such as carpeted entranceways, elevators, stairs, and the carpet in front of tellers in banks.

4) Overall cleaning of carpet for deep hot water extraction. The four steps covered in this maintenance program are all covered in Chapter III. The frequency of these four steps in carpet maintenance vary tremendously. For example: a school system will 1) vacuum daily, 2) remove spillage as it occurs daily, weekly and monthly, 3) perform bonnet buffing in the heavy traffic areas, nightly, weekly and monthly as necessary and 4) perform hot water extraction twice a year at the Christmas holidays and at the June closing. Naturally, the interim maintenance is greatly affected by the weather conditions in the areas where the school is located. Another example, gambling casinos will bonnet buff only and might not use any other method, due to the drying time involved.

In conclusion, each separate building must establish its own frequency for the four maintenance steps required. Most sanitary supply distributors are quite capable of recommending methods, chemicals and machines to be used for these various maintenance steps.

CHAPTER VII

FUTURE OF ON-LOCATION CARPET MAINTENANCE PREDICTIONS BY EXECUTIVES OF NINE SPONSORING COMPANIES OF THIS BOOKLET

The nine sponsoring companies of this book are leading manufacturers and suppliers to the maintenance supply trade of carpet cleaning equipment, supplies and chemicals. As the publisher Reinecke Associates requested, an executive of each of these nine companies is providing a short statement pertaining to the future of on-location carpet cleaning, as we enter the last half of the 80's and the 90's.

Tom VanderBie, Executive Vice-President
Castex Industries, Inc.
Holland, MI 49423

Carpet maintenance is nearing the end of a controversial period. Old techniques and ideas are now riding backseat to the new high-tech methods of today. The transitional period has been one that spanned three decades, pitting industry rivals against not only each other, but the uncertainty of proper maintenance techniques.

From the "Black Magic" of yesterday, carpet cleaning techniques and machines have evolved to a scientific level. This new stage has eliminated the guess work from carpet cleaning. Now a level of consistency is being maintained throughout the industry.

The past five years have seen carpet maintenance take huge strides in progress. Equipment has advanced across the board in quality, reliability and performance. Scientific techniques have put an end to the old myths that once ruled our industry. Manufacturers provided not only the most innovative equipment, but equally important education programs on proper machine usage and carpet mainte-

43

nance. End users now have unlimited access to training from manufacturers and distributors. The combined efforts of both have stabilized the uncertainties of carpet maintenance. Equipment of today is much easier to use and requires less exertion from the operator. The use of on-location self-contained hot water extraction carpet cleaning machines are much easier to use, reducing the fatigue factor, and adding to the efficiency of the employee. In addition, automatics have reduced overall maintenance costs allowing for areas to be maintained more often and still remain cost effective. Machinery has advanced to the point where operator error is minimal. Future success will greatly depend on our ability to continue improving communication, pursue higher levels of professionalism, and relentlessly concentrate our efforts on education. The unification of maintenance techniques between equipment manufacturers and carpet mills will require a major undertaking, but will prove valuable to all concerned. A concentrated effort must be put forth to achieve this goal. The carpet segment of the sanitary supply industry looks to have a great future. Manufacturers, mills and sanitary supply distributors should all prosper.

Gordon S. Clausen, President
Clausen Marketing Associates
Bryn Mawr, PA 19010

The late 80's and 90's will encounter an explosion in carpet maintenance. With increased population, increased housing, increased schools, buildings, hospitals, etc., carpet will be the leading floor covering in the future. Several important factors will even become more important in the future of carpet maintenance. Number one will be the cost of cleaning. With ever increasing labor costs, the methods that produce the best cleaning with the lowest cost will predominate. Three factors determine the cost of cleaning: A) The number of labor steps required, B) The number of machines required, and C) The chemical costs. We, therefore, predict that rotary bonnet buffing with its low labor cost and one chemical will completely dominate interim carpet maintenance. For the same reasons hot water extraction with brush heads will completely dominate overall deep periodic cleaning. For large acreage of carpet, the new automatic carpet scrubbers will be an absolute must.

Gone will be the days when carpet was cleaned only and additional costs were charged for such chemical services as deodorizing or sanitizing the carpet. With the Environmental Protection Agency approval, the sanitizers and deodorizers will be added to the cleaning chemicals in order to accomplish all three, cleaning, sanitizing and deodorizing in one labor step cleaning, such as; bonnet buffing or hot water extraction. Note: For quaternary ammonias to accomplish Environmental Protection Agency registered sanitizing, it requires the presence of moisture and water, therefore, eliminating powder dry cleaners as sanitizing agents. Carpet protectors in order to be as effective as possible, will still require the dirty carpet to be completely hot water extracted before applying protectors as an additional labor step.

Gary Gradinger, President
Golden Star, Inc.
N. Kansas City, MO 64116

As the only primary manufacturer of *both* carpeting and bonnet cleaning systems sponsoring this booklet, Golden Star has a rather unique perspective of on-location carpet maintenance. As a carpet mill, we are acutely aware that one of the greatest deterrents to the growth of carpeting is ineffective and costly maintenance. Just as individuals expect the "wet look" in hard surface flooring at an economical cost, they likewise demand continually clean carpets, performed quickly and economically. Bonnet cleaning satisfies their need especially in high traffic areas between

45

extraction cleanings.

Accelerating the growth of bonnet systems in the future are innovations in the pad itself including permanently impregnated anti-microbials to eliminate mildew and bacterial growth, sophisticated yarn blends for greater absorption and durability, and construction enhancements for aggressive performance and longer life. Value best describes the bonnet system and projects a very promising future for this method of on-location cleaning.

John F. Bevington, President
National Super Service Co.
Maumee, OH 43537

National Super Service Company has been involved in the sale of cold water extraction machines since 1972, and in hot water extraction machines since 1977. In addition, we have had significant success in selling 300 rpm single-disc machines, for bonnet cleaning. Our recommendations for a carpet cleaning program today—to be successful is:

• Daily Vacuuming
• Monthly Bonnet Cleaning, At High Speeds (i.e., 300 RPMS) of all traffic areas.
• Water Cleaning Of All Walk-Off Mats, and Heavy Traffic Areas at Entrances and Exits
• Extraction of Total Carpet At Least Twice a Year

There is no substitute for wet extraction cleaning. There is no competing method for thoroughness of cleaning, without residue. So-called "dry cleaning" method of carpets is slow, costly, and offers unsatisfactory results—particularly in appearance (residue is left in the carpet). As a consequence, our prediction for the future is that on a competitive basis with any other type of carpet maintenance, the use of on-location portable hot water extraction machines will grow. This will be the result of more efficient machines, and better trained operators to protect the valuable investment in carpeting.

46

Ted C. Moss, President
Seco Industries, Inc.
Cleveland, Tennessee

Seco Industries feels that Spin Klean® bonnet cleaning will grow as a popular on-location carpet maintenance method. Factors contributing to this growth will include the rise in labor costs, labor turnover, the demand for thorough, frequent carpet cleaning in high traffic areas and a general attitude trend toward preventive carpet maintenance. Unlike many other methods, Spin Klean® bonnet cleaning requires no specialized equipment, extensive operator training and, overall, is among the lowest cost systems to use. Thus more commercial end users can afford to interim maintain their carpets. Seco feels the bonnet cleaning method is being increasingly accepted as an all-around carpet maintenance system.

Seco also feels that evolution in the end-user marketplace will also contribute to the growth of bonnet carpet cleaning. Convention centers, twenty-four hour restaurants, theaters, hotels, airports and other facilities with high-traffic carpeted areas are on the increase. Bonnet cleaning has a natural place in these environments.

Dana K. Griffin, President
Tu Way Products Co.
Rockford, OH 45882

The growing use of carpeting as a floor covering adds emphasis to the need for a well executed maintenance system.

Until the recent past, there was no credible system in place. So, carpeting was permitted to be "soiled to death" with the expectation that a miraculous resurrection could take place. Well, it could take place, but most of the time it hits the pocketbook with the cost impact of a new carpet.

The bonnet system of preventive maintenance, when properly and frequently performed, keeps the carpet "looking new." That's because it does an excellent job of cleaning the carpet surface—takes only minutes to do—and a few more minutes to dry. The cost is proportionately low.

It does not "deep clean" but neither do the eyes "deep see." This extra depth of cleaning must be accomplished by a quality vacuum cleaner. This maintenance system of bonnet cleaning combined with quality vacuum cleaning will let your carpet grow old with the appearance of youth.

Edward B. Buchanan, Vice President
Vestal Laboratories, Inc.
(Subsidiary of Chemed Corp.)
St. Louis, MO 63110

The growth of carpeting in the health care industry, i.e., hospitals, nursing care units, etc., in recent years has been astounding. Carpeting has been installed in locations we never thought possible several years ago such as critical care units. This brings one to think of the possibility of infection with the lack of germicide use where carpet covered surfaces exist. There has to be concern. Vestal Laboratories, firmly entrenched in the health care market, feels that without killing the problem-causing bacteria, there is the possibility of cross infection. This can be partially controlled with quality cleaning equipment, chemicals, and procedures. However, it still leaves doubt of total bacteria control.

Educational facilities have been another rapid growth areas for carpet use, and some of the same concerns and problems exist. Many times the surface may not be properly cleaned or attended to as the need may occur, once again bringing to mind an effective sanitizing product used in the maintenance procedure.

Products are currently being developed and the near future will bring quality EPA approved germicidal and sanitizing carpet cleaning agents. With these new products, then and only then, can we add to the ensuring of proper infection control.

Carpeting will remain the fastest growing floor covering,

and with this, issues the challenge to our industry to maintain state of the art cleaning equipment and chemicals to meet the needs of our changing environment.

Richard E. Whittaker, President
R. D. Whitaker Co.
Newcaste, PA 16103

Commercial carpet cleaning in the 90's will be *done on an almost daily basis* in schools, hospitals and industries, etc. It doesn't make sense to do "Restoration" type cleaning on an annual or semi-annual basis, when recent studies seem to support that if you wait too long to clean, you might, at best, only get out 15% of the dirt trapped in the carpet. Therefore, machines such as Roto Wash, which are fast and easy to use, leave no residue and also pile lift will become the dominant force in the maintenance of carpet.

I predict, that in most locations, washing and pile lifting the carpet will be done every-other-day in conjunction with a sound vacuuming program. Institutions that are now using this system have been able to keep on top of their cleaning requirements.

There is no question that the sale of carpeting and carpet squares will be increasing yearly. Anyone involved with cleaning carpeting should make a study of the different methods available, so that they will have the knowledge to choose what system is best for their needs.

Charles Hasper, Vice-President
Windsor Industries
Englewood, Colorado
Equipment sold as Mr. Steem

"The term 'on-location carpet maintenance' tells us a great deal about where the carpet cleaning industry finds itself today. First of all, nearly all carpet cleaning is now done 'on-location,' and secondly, 'carpet maintenance' has become the key to our future. A successful future lies with the company that can provide equipment to maintain carpet at its highest level of cleanliness in the shortest possible time. Every day, acres of carpet are being installed in new commercial buildings, and many more acres of hard surface floors are being covered with carpet in existing buildings. The key to the future is faster and better cleaning of these large carpeted areas, and the extraction process is the only way to do it efficiently.

Our company is dedicated to the concept of high-speed carpet extraction with the resulting lowest labor cost."

REINECKE ASSOCIATES
Box 3112
West Chester, PA 19380

Please send me_____copies of "CARPET PROCURE-MENT & MAINTENANCE FOR THE NINETIES @ $5.00 per copy.*

I enclose my check or money order (not cash) in the amount of $_____to cover the order.

*Pennsylvania residents add applicable sales tax.

NAME_____

ADDRESS_____

_____

_____

TELE. NO. (   )_____

NOTES

NOTES

NOTES

Today Polypropaline to be used as prim + secondary Backing

Dupont — Stainmaster

Monsanto — Stain Blocker

Allied Chemide — Anso 5 worste free.

NOTES

NOTES